WE NEED CHANGE

Norman J. Allen

DEDICATION

This book is dedicated to those who keep trying to create a dialogue with those who think differently. To those who believe that, in the end, we need friendships and understanding.

This book is also dedicated to those patiently trying to make the world around them a better place. It is a difficult path but definitely worth it.

So, keep going.

TABLE OF CONTENTS

ACKNOWLEDGEMENTS 5

INTRODUCTION 6

Chapter 01 9

Chapter 02 15

Chapter 03 20

Chapter 04 27

Chapter 05 34

Chapter 06 43

Chapter 07 48

Chapter 08 | CONCLUSION 52

ACKNOWLEDGEMENTS

I would like to express gratitude to all of my former students who took part in my class by presenting questions. Your participation in the conversations has had a significant impact on my viewpoint of the world around me and contributed, in part, to the creation of this book.

INTRODUCTION

"A lot of problems in the world would be solved if we talked to each other instead of about each other."

— *Nicky Gumbel*

As someone who teaches high school social studies, I am frequently questioned about our society and the issues that are plaguing it. This is such a loaded question! There are a lot of things going on all at once, and most of them are connected to one another in some way. Since I've been in this profession for a significant amount of time, I frequently run across some of my old pupils. In addition to talking about the good old days and catching up on how things are going in their lives, they frequently express regret for their behavior in class years prior. Regardless of the fact that I like the sentiment, I find it to be all too indicative of some of the most significant challenges that we face as a society. There is a general lack of regard for people who are trying to educate us on how our Republic is "supposed to work," and we do not pay attention to our history; we do not take things like learning about the Constitution seriously.

It has never been my intention to indoctrinate teenagers or to try to shape their thinking in a certain direction; rather, all I want to do is help them in becoming more knowledgeable. However, after teaching for more than ten years, I came to the conclusion that the issue is not just of youngsters having a negative attitude about school; rather, the issue is much more fundamental. Our country has a problem with the manner in which we regard education, our past, as well as the way in which we view and respect one another. On top of that, we are positive that we are the only ones who are aware of the truth and that everyone else is in the wrong.

6

It is essential for us to have a conversation. In point of fact, all of us could use a talk, and the entire United States of America would benefit much from taking a moment to relax, breathe deeply, and resume their discourse. We used to communicate with one another, and we used to be people who were good at finding solutions to problems, but I fear that we have lost our way. In today's world, many of us are quick to take offense or feel like we've been victimized, and as a result, we may feel inclined to respond with a more harsh attitude that does not really reflect our upbringing or our genuine intelligence. This is not to argue that there are no situations in which we have a right to react, but there are times when it is just the reality that we no longer demonstrate patience and understanding when it comes to social and political challenges. When it comes to ideological differences, there used to be a lot of people who held the belief that people should just live and let others live their lives, but those days are long gone.

This book is a humble attempt to get people to reflect on the way that we as a society think about things. In this short book, I have discussed a few of the topics that I believe should be brought up in conversation right away in order to assist us in determining how we may bring about change. In my opinion, we as a nation have become completely lost. We have reached a point where we are no longer able to speak through our differences and find solutions to the problems that we face; as a result, we are currently standing on the precipice of social upheaval or maybe something even more severe.

In order to restart the conversation, we need to figure out how to get it going again. For me, a concert by Roger Waters and a lot of people talking about how we are not communicating and placing our confidence in the wrong places were the impetus to begin my journey. It got me thinking; have we developed an unhealthy level of trust in our political leaders? Why do

7

we react so much to what the media shows when the vast majority of us are in agreement that the media cannot be trusted? What can we do to change the current situation?

I have dredged up some problems that are prevalent in today's society, as well as in the classroom, the home, and the workplace, among many other places. I believe that we live in an amazing country; nevertheless, our nation is plagued with issues, and if we want to make things better, I believe that we need to take a hard look at ourselves first. We need to be honest with ourselves, and we need to be willing to communicate with each other in order to work through our issues and perhaps rediscover why we once respected certain individuals but no longer do so. We have to begin our endeavors at some point, and the now is as good a moment as any other to do so.

"To effectively communicate, we must realize that we are all different in the way we perceive the world and use this understanding as a guide to our communication with others."

— *Anthony Robbins*

Please take all of this with a grain of salt and keep in mind that we are going to have various opinions on these topics as well as different values regarding what is essential to us in the present moment. There are a great many contributing factors that influence us, such as our culture, our religious origins, our families, our education, and so on. But if we can find out how to make some changes to our society, we might be able to escape some of the gloomy forecasts that people are making for the United States of America and have hope for a better future.

CHAPTER 01

We need change.

How many times have we heard this line before? Has it actually changed anything yet? We always demand change but do we really believe that people can change? That's a question that is always there in our subconscious. If only we took some time out of our schedules and actually pondered over it.

And the majority of people who do think about it come to the conclusion that the answer is "no." Throughout the years, I have heard a lot of people say that people don't actually change. Ironic, given that at the same time, they expect a change in behavior on the part of others when they find themselves in a situation involving some kind of conflict. Which one is it, then? Is it possible for individuals to change, and if so, what are the prerequisites for changing the mindsets of an entire population of people?

These are the concepts that I want to discuss in this book. Why? Because I believe everyone needs change and demands it. But the real problem begins when they are questioned about how we bring about that change. How do we persuade 330 million people to reconsider the way that they think about themselves and the other people in their surroundings? That includes individuals who they do not like, people who are wealthy and people who are poor, and people of diverse races and ethnic origins to change their viewpoint in regard to economics, history, politics, and society in general. Pretty exhausting, no?

As an advocate for change, I do not pretend to have the answers, but I do believe that there is one way to get all of us on the right track, and that way is to communicate with one another. At the very least, this constitutes the important first step. It is not enough for us to simply be willing to talk about all of these topics; we also need to be willing to listen to what other people have to say.

During the course of my life, I have witnessed how individuals gradually become more isolated within echo chambers when it comes to matters of politics, economics, and general societal problems. I can think of a few reasons why this could have happened. I recall learning about how home construction in the United States has changed as a result of the proliferation of televisions in American households and the subsequent decline in people's participation in neighborhood social activities. If you find an older house that was constructed before the 1970s, there is a good chance that it has a sizable porch area. This is often where you will find people lounging and relaxing and even catching up with friends, family, and other neighbors.

How often do you see that now?

As the television became more prominent in our homes, porches got smaller, and living rooms and family rooms became larger to accommodate sitting around the TV. People have, since about that time, started to be less sociable with their neighbors and less interactive with their communities. This may have been the point where it all started; the gap and the lack of. From that point on, as a result of the diversification of our entertainment and music, we started to diversify more of who we were. This is not a bad thing, but perhaps we went a little bit too far with it. Think back to the movies that we have all seen, notably the ones about high school and the fact that there are always different groups and cliques. The majority of these cliques either do not interact with certain other groups or view those other groups in a negative light for some reason. It's funny and dramatic, but I can't help but believe that we've

10

conditioned ourselves to be segregated into "like-minded" groups. We assess the worth of individuals based on what sort of group they belong to, and I feel that this is a contributing factor to the problem that we have. Then we convince ourselves that they are incapable of understanding us and that we are similarly unable to understand them.

On occasion, I will see content creators discussing this topic and how "they" want us to be separated so we cannot concentrate on the actual problems that are happening in the United States of America. I have a strong hunch that this is true, yet I am unable to identify "they." It is likely that there is no one watching over this, but that we, the people, are the ones who are creating and perpetuating these circumstances. We give credence to the notion that differences in our racial and cultural backgrounds, as well as our economic and religious ideals, prevent us from having meaningful relationships with one another.

The more I discover about other people and their cultures, the more I realize that, at our core, we are all looking for the same things. We want to be happy, we want to be respected, we want to be successful, loved, and appreciated, and we want to be able to provide for our families and ensure a bright future for them. The way in which we carry this out and the criteria we use to evaluate our success is, however, completely different. Being different is completely okay, and there is nothing wrong with being different. However, when we devalue other groups just because they approach issues in a different way, we run the risk of causing problems.

I do not feel qualified to talk about race relations and the problems that we still have with racism and prejudice. Perhaps we still need to talk about this subject, even though it makes us feel uncomfortable. As an educator, I've discovered that the

11

experiences I've had in the classroom have taught me that different people have various conceptions of what racism is and how reparation ought to be carried out in the event that someone engages in behavior that is biased or racist. I have also realized that overt expressions of hatred, violence, or rhetoric are not the only way to be racist and that racism may take more hidden forms. I have enough good judgment to see that people are sick of listening to white guys talk about racism and how to change it. I personally have been through listening to a fair proportion of them. Again, how are we ever going to make any headway on these issues if we stop communicating with one another and/or listening to one another?

Back to square one.

We need to find a way to reopen the channels of communication with tolerance and compassion for one another, and we need to listen to one another while we do so. The different life experiences that each of us has resulted in the development of our own points of view. Where I grew up, I had very few interactions with the police, and in my whole life, I have only once or twice felt that law enforcement officials mistreated me. If you are willing to seek, you may come across a plethora of stories of minorities living in urban regions who have had many awful experiences. In many cases, they have been in our national media. If you are ready to look, you can find these stories.

You have to keep one thing in mind in regard to the media: they are businesses, and in order to generate money, they need readers and viewers. Nothing will draw viewers more quickly than the display of the worst character let loose in public. We can't truly change what the media does, but we can change how we react to the things we see in the media. The media will continue to do what they do. We have all heard this before. But it needs to be stated; we cannot change the world; however, starting with ourselves, we can change the way in which we perceive the world.

One effective way to go about it is that when things like this happen, we must wait for the whole story. This element of the challenge, the waiting game, is by far the most difficult. We need to be ready to wait for the release of proof, such as body cam footage or any other authentic evidence because that is where the truth lies. In the first few minutes, or even the first few hours or days after an incident has taken place, we are never privy to the entire story.

There is something that can be done to help with this situation, and that is for us to put pressure on our political leaders and law enforcement officers, particularly those who are in leadership roles, to ensure that body cam footage, video evidence, and other such things are made available to the media and the general public in a timely manner.

In certain instances, it would appear that the general public is required to wait for too long, and the harm has already been done. As a result, trust in our judicial system is further weakened. Both in terms of how we interact with ourselves and with the people in authority above us, we as a society need to do better at what we do. We put up with poor leadership or a complete absence of leadership until the situation reaches a critical point, where at times, we lash out. When it comes down to it, we are the ones who will be on the hook for the costs associated with the destruction of our cities. When federal agencies or other groups supported by the government utilize federal money, they are using tax dollars, which is money that we pay as part of our annual financial obligations. When something like this happens, there is no denying that a message is being conveyed. But in retrospect, is it the message we want to send?

CHAPTER 02

"There can be no faith in government if our highest offices are excused from scrutiny - they should be setting the example of transparency."

-Edward Snowden

Transparency guarantees the availability of information that can be utilized to evaluate the functioning of the authorities and to protect against any potential abuse of power. In this view, transparency serves as a tool to establish accountability, which implies that authorities may very well be held responsible for the activities that they undertake. It is impossible for a government to earn the trust of the people it rules if it does not practice accountability and transparency. The ultimate outcome would be societal instability and a culture that is not particularly favorable to the development of the country.

There was a time the media's presence in the political world was a significant way of accountability for leaders' actions. Since the public no longer has a great level of trust in the media, there have been changes made in the way that failures in the government are confronted. Appointed and administrative authorities are often held to a lesser bar of accountability than elected officials. The size of the federal government determines the scope of legislative scrutiny provided by Congress. The 535 members of Congress are responsible for exercising legislative oversight over the agencies. The Federal Register now contains information about 445 different agencies. This results in an average of 1.2 congressional representatives serving each agency.

Executive officers are required to accept responsibility for individuals who report to them; yet, executive officers are frequently underpaid and overworked, which means that they do not have the time to supervise the employees' day-to-day responsibilities. This scenario does not take into account the fact that the majority of political corruption happens at the most senior levels of the organization. The recent political situation has demonstrated that our present and previous governments not only cover up the failings of people in their inner circle but also conceal those failures from the general public. The general public continues to be entirely misled or uneducated regarding public policy, which results in a failure of their ability to make judgments that are in the best interest of the country.

Source: https://patimes.org/accountability-and-transparency-in-public-administration/

What is the solution? Those who abuse their authority, including those in positions of political or legal leadership, who are caught committing crimes need to be held responsible, and this has to happen in a timely manner. There should be no delays that can be avoided in the first place. This is not a very simple task; however, our judicial system does include time limits in order to ensure that an accused person is tried in an appropriate manner. Just because we think someone is guilty does not make it so. Everyone, not only the people we happen to admire, have the right to a trial that is handled fairly. The only way to restore the trust of the public in our judicial system is to operate in a fully open and transparent manner. Up until then, it is likely that they will never feel it is their system, and until then, we will continue to see divisions widening among the populace.

To put it bluntly and simply, we need to get people talking again. We have to be capable of listening to constructive criticism and engaging in conversation about the state of our society. I have a feeling that we have lost the ability to accept criticism from other people. Perhaps we were never very good at it, but I believe that the moment has come for us to start listening to what other people have to say. This is not an invitation to say whatever you want and however you want. Regardless of how inviting it may be, this should not be construed as such. Yes, we must own our shortcomings and be open to constructive criticism, but we need to also acquire the skills necessary to have a conversation with another person and provide feedback without belittling them as individuals.

The government needs to know that despite all the shortcomings, they must let the public know of their affairs to build trust. Citizens have an inherent right to know the truth about public affairs, and it is the responsibility of the government to guarantee that this right is upheld. This is what we mean when we talk about transparency. Greater methods of secrecy and more knowledge that is meant to be kept hidden are available to administrators and politicians than to members of any other profession. False opinions and statistics are frequently spread across public discourse with the intention of distracting people from learning certain truths. If you are educated about law or government, you will be able to gather information on things like rules, legislative sessions, and other such topics. In light of the aforementioned, public administrators are obligated to provide any and all information that pertains to the organization that they supervise. Serving the public is supposed to be one of the main goals of public administration. In the case that the information gathered by that agency is not made available to the general public, the quality of the service relationship will suffer.

It doesn't matter who you are or what party or position you hold; if we genuinely want to bring about change and make it lasting, we need to have more tolerance for the ways in which people are different than us. As someone who specializes in education, I have had the opportunity to listen to several highly educated professionals discuss societal issues and present their point of view as though they had been given a mandate from on high to enlighten masses who just do not know anything about the subject. If we can't even treat other people with respect, how can we expect them to listen to what we have to say? You see, it works both ways. If you want to be listened to, you have to listen to others as well. That's how a conversation goes.

I get asked from time to time, how do I deal with teenagers who are ignorant or otherwise uninformed on the topic we are on in class? The answer is rather straightforward: since I am a teacher, this presents me with a chance to teach. If I make the student feel stupid, then the chance to educate them is lost, and it is likely that they will remember the negative aspects of that interaction for many years to come. It will be more effective if

I communicate with them on their level, try to assist them in recognizing where they are wrong, show them in a positive way, and reinforce the notion with greater understanding. It is an even more powerful teaching moment if I am able to help them autonomously recognize the consequence or come up with the appropriate response. If we want to have a positive impact on others around us and help them in seeing things from a new point of view, we need to share our knowledge with them in a constructive manner and avoid making them feel as if they are worthless just because they have a different opinion.

For me, the fact that I am an introvert is a great irony in this scenario. It nearly seems like hypocrisy on my part to recommend something with which I myself struggle and that I frequently choose not to do. But, I am smart enough to realize that I need to make this change in myself. It is important for me to overcome my social tendencies to sit in the back, and one of the ways I am doing so is by writing this, whatever it is. In point of fact, it goes much further than that; I need to make sure I always respect other people, even when we have major differences. It is essential for me to be actively listening to and participating in the events taking place around me. I believe that there are a lot of people who are under the impression that they do not have to become involved and that they would rather not have conversations about sensitive topics, but we have to. It is imperative that we allow ourselves to take part in social dialogues; it is only through discussion that we will be able to overcome our differences and become closer to one another.

CHAPTER 03

"When you give everyone a voice and give people power, the system usually ends up in a really good place. So, what we view our role as, is giving people that power."

-Mark Zuckerberg

The power of one's voice can take us into the future as no other tool can. A future that is filled with more opportunities and more ways to solve problems. It is a tool that can be utilized for stepping up for what is right instead of what is easy, and it offers your thoughts a platform and presents you with the chance to have perspective and understanding on issues that matter.

There are no two voices that are identical; rather, every voice has something unique to convey. And in a world that must stand for liberty and democracy, the strength of one's own voice is a potent representation of this necessity. It is what has made it possible for people to speak out against injustice, sing songs of liberation, and even just speak the truth. When things are difficult, having a voice could be a source of encouragement.

Change can be brought about by using our voices. We are supposed to inspire others to use their words as well, to come together, and to support one another.

The misperception is that one must be popular or have a thousand followers in order to be able to empower another person or make a difference in society. Neither of these prerequisites is necessary. No matter how old or young you are, you can make a difference in the lives of people in communities all over the world by contributing in a number of ways, both big and small, by using your voice to advocate for positive change.

I would like to speak about an experience that helped me have a deeper appreciation for the freedom that comes with speaking one's views. On September 8, 2022, I had the privilege of going to see Roger Waters, of Pink Floyd fame, in Salt Lake City. Since I was in the middle of my junior year of high school, I have been admiring Pink Floyd and Roger Waters' solo work. I have only recently been familiar with Roger Waters' political ideas, and to tell you the truth, when I first read about them, they created quite a bit of surprise and confusion in my mind. I had several friends who were originally from the United Kingdom, and I had also spent some time living there, so I was somewhat familiar with the kind of liberalism that is prevalent in that country.

There were two announcements made right before the concert started. The first one asked everyone to silence their cellphones so that they could all get the most out of the show. The second one suggested that if you enjoy the music but cannot stomach Roger's politics, you should relocate yourself "kindly" to the nearby bar. And that was the one that caught my attention more entirely. I couldn't help but laugh and clap my hands as I anticipated being presented with some novel concepts. I had no idea how unfamiliar these ideas would be to me, nor was I aware of the context in which they would be presented. The way Roger weaved his politics into the music that he performed, in addition to the way that the visuals and other forms of media exhibited on the screens, reinforced his message. Perhaps this is why they were meaningful to me.

After a while, in the breaks between songs, Roger took a moment at the piano and started talking to all of us, almost in the same way that I occasionally talk to my students. That is something that I truly admire. I have no doubt that Roger is wealthy, and you have this preconceived notion that famous people, due to their elevated status, carry themselves in a particular way that makes them appear to be from a higher station in life as if they are better than you. With Roger, on the other hand, this was not the case at all. He didn't sugarcoat anything, and he did it in such a manner that it made me feel as though we were just a group of friends sitting around, and Roger decided to stop by for a quick chat.

What stuck out to me the most was the way he referred to the piano and the stage as a bar. He said that we were all here to chat and listen (or something like that), and I got the impression that what he was saying was genuine. I did not get the feeling that he was an elite trying to impose his viewpoint on us; rather, I got the impression that he had a unique point of view that was worth considering. To reiterate, was I completely in agreement with everything I read or heard throughout that night? No, but he got me thinking, and he had me questioning not just what I thought I understood but also why I embraced the ideologies that I had. Although I didn't relate to the entirety of Roger's message, I can't deny that he was a driving force behind my introspection and growth. His ideas on communication stuck out the most to me, and I believed that we should have more dialogues.

I have been exposed to some quite radical concepts in the past, and it is likely that the manner in which they were conveyed was liable for the reactions I had to them. Perhaps it is the fact that I am a middle-aged man who has become exhausted from working in a system that appears to be so severely controlled that not many individuals make it very far anymore. My time in college and the few years that followed were spent actively participating in American politics as a Democrat. However, I eventually became disillusioned due to their message and political practices, which seemed to thrive off the idea that they truly cared about people in general and minorities in particular. I think I just couldn't figure out where exactly my place was and ended up going from party to party looking for it.

Ultimately, I discovered that I needed to refresh my understanding of what George Washington had said in his farewell address on the different political parties. In essence, Washington advised that we should steer clear of political parties, alliances, and other forms of political entanglements, saying that they were not a good idea. I have observed how our political parties let the people of the United States of America down, and I am sure that many others would agree with me on this point. There are a large number of people living in the United States right now who have expressed similar concerns regarding our political parties and the way in which our politicians make promises to both sides of the political spectrum but then, once they are in office, they do whatever they want and rarely follow through on their commitments to represent their local population.

Many individuals on all sides of the political spectrum have expressed frustration to me about what they see as a lack of representation on the part of their political leaders and representatives, and I have heard their concerns. It does appear as though they had "some kind of schema" in place, according to which they will vote most of the time in accordance with the expectations of the party, but they will deviate from party lines on occasion. We hear the most about this from Republicans, who refer to those who act in this manner as RINOs (which stands for "Republican in name only") and frequently voice their dissatisfaction with those individuals. To become familiar with the Constitution, we need to educate ourselves on the powers that are held by the various branches of government. If I were to argue for anything, it would be that our allegiance ought to be to the Constitution and not to political parties. I am aware that political parties are able to garner support for particular candidates; however, it is precisely this kind of undying allegiance and reliance that gives rise to the "Us versus Them" dynamic. In this case, the party in question will always be the heroes, while the opposing party will always play the role of the villains.

I moved to Utah when I was around 15 years old, and I remember learning about political parties toward the end of high school. Many of my friends would joke that the R is for righteousness and the D is for devils. It has become second nature for us to subdivide our population and organize ourselves into smaller groups or clans; thus, should it come as any surprise that our country still struggles with issues of prejudice and racism in the 21st century? It almost appears as though as we get closer to each new stage in our life, we figure out who we will get along with, become friends with them, and label everyone else as our adversary. If we are always seeking new ways to exclude and marginalize one another, how can our society ever make strides toward a more just and inclusive future?

The primaries are the ones who incur the most harm as a result of this. Why do you ask? To participate in a primary election in many states, you are required to be a member of the political party in question. Therefore, at the most fundamental level, only the most dedicated party members vote, or in other situations, you have individuals who just enrolled in that party but are not actively supporting that party, which, in most cases, does not do much to affect the outcome of the election. When the time comes to cast votes, it goes without saying that every registered voter has the right to vote for anybody they like. We need to give some thought to altering the way in which we enable primary elections to take place and heeding the counsel of George Washington to do away with political parties. We have also allowed the rules and procedures around elections to become so onerous that it would be difficult for the average adult to have any chance of standing for political office. When we take a look at the Constitution, we find that there are very few requirements for our political offices. When I taught government, my students were often surprised to see how little qualifications are needed to hold the post of president. However, we make it appear as though it is practically impossible, particularly when you consider the amount of money that is spent during each election cycle, and you see why only the wealthiest people in the United States run for government.

At this point, you can be excused for wondering, what exactly does Roger Waters' concert have to do with political parties? It has to do with one of the first phrases I saw displayed during the show: "Who tells us who is good and who is bad?"

The answer to this question is "the government," and it is conveyed to us through the channel of our choosing (the media). We are still being told who the good guys and bad guys are, and this happens irrespective of whether the source is CNN, Fox News, or any other source. This has never been more obvious than it was in 2016 when everyone responded differently to the news that Donald Trump had been elected president. One thing is certain: Washington, D.C., and every media source were repeatedly trying to tell you how you needed to think and feel about Trump being president and how you needed to feel and think about those who supported him and those who were against him. You may love him, you may hate him, and we could go on forever about that. In point of fact, people are still arguing over this topic two years after Joseph Biden was elected president, and the media is actively pushing on behalf of both sides of the debate.

This was not precisely where Roger was heading with his statement; I am certain he was referring to global issues, namely how our government takes sides on issues and then pushes for that support here at home. Nevertheless, I believe that this is a great point at which to begin. The conflict over the dissemination of information has been going on for far more than six years at this point, and its scope extends well beyond the realm of events happening in other countries.

CHAPTER 04

"If people in the media cannot decide whether they are in the business of reporting news or manufacturing propaganda, it is all the more important that the public understand that difference and choose their news sources accordingly."

-Thomas Sowell

I am not implying that the media is a negative thing in any way. However, taking into account the ways in which it is redefining how to report and the contents that it publishes and broadcasts, it is high time to reflect on a few facts that the general public may not have been paying attention to. The dissemination of information is one of the primary functions of the media, but in today's hyper-connected world, information moves far more quickly than "facts" and "the truth." And many times, information is only half the truth or still needs to be sorted before concluding anything.

Both the news media and the government are involved in a vicious cycle of mutual self-interest, mythmaking, and brainwashing of the public. Crises are crucial for journalists to add drama to the news, and government leaders give the impression that they are responding to crises. All too frequently, the crises in question are not genuine crises but rather the fabrications of many parties. Both the government and the news media have gotten so entangled in a mutually reinforcing web of deception that neither can successfully communicate the truth to the general public. This leaves both institutions powerless to rule in an efficient manner.

These days, and for the past few years, the media doesn't report the news as facts and truth. They twist things and present them in a way that affects the way their audience thinks. They do not report the news of an event but rather "tell" them how to see and think about a certain subject or event.

And that's where all the problem begins.

Should the government and the media be the ones to tell us who the good and the bad people are, or should they instead be the ones to provide the facts and let us, the people, come to our own conclusions based on what we know?

Both the news media and the government have concocted an elaborate hoax in order to encourage their respective agendas while deceiving the general population. As a result of the officials' willingness to generate crises and carefully stage-manage their answers, they are able to increase both their own status and authority in the public's eyes. Journalists, according to their profession, faithfully report on those lies and distortions. Both sides are aware that the stories are manipulations designed to promote their own self-interest and fail to enlighten the public on the more important but less interesting aspects of government policy and activities.

Ronald Regan said something that has been profound for me as an educator:

"Freedom is never more than one generation away from extinction."

This is quite the statement to make. The comment made by Regan is succinct yet insightful, considering that in our Republic, we demand participation from our citizens, and in order to participate effectively, one has to be informed. I would say that this extends beyond only paying attention in school to also include paying attention to what is going on in the community, the nation, and the world. How else are you going to be able to develop opinions and choose courses of action about the events that are taking place in our world? If our government and media are attempting to influence how you think, even if they think they are doing it for the greater good by distorting information, they are still trying to manipulate how you think. If you do not believe me, check the polls; I believe that we have allowed our leaders, whom we do not trust to govern, to dictate how we think. If you do not believe me, I believe that we have gotten too comfortable with this system.

As a teacher, I have witnessed a great number of teenagers get disheartened as a result of witnessing the disparity between what America was intended to be and what it really is. You can address this from a number of different angles. My view is that the United States of America is a concept and that the Constitution is the document in which that idea lives and thrives. You can see how numerous leaders at all levels of government have used the Constitution to serve their goals, and this is true regardless of which political party you support. It is not that the Constitution itself needs to be amended but rather how we interpret the Constitution. To begin, one of the most significant problems that we have is that a very small percentage of the population is even aware of what is written in the Constitution, which branches of government hold specific authorities, etc.

When I used to teach government to seniors in high school, I would quote Abraham Lincoln to my students "The Constitution must be our political religion." In my opinion, I feel that this statement is grossly overlooked. When we, as a part of a Republic, want to be able to make informed judgments when we vote and support politicians, we need to be conversant with our Constitution. Although I make an effort not to be a conspiracy theorist and to not entertain wild thoughts any more than a person should, there are times when it seems as though people in political power would rather their population stay ignorant. If any of this is true, then obviously, this is something that should be resisted at all costs. In light of the present circumstances, a few different possibilities are conceivable. People are going to give up on the system and not engage because they are disillusioned by the lack of representation, even if it is just a perception that it is lacking representation. This only assists those individuals within a party who are considered more radical to get elected and get through the primary. As a nation, we have an obligation to get knowledgeable about our Constitution and to cease allowing outsiders to interpret it for us and to offer promises that they are either unable or unwilling to keep.

This may seem like a daunting task. How exactly am I expected to get educated about the Constitution? It will not occur all at once, and it may even take you a very long time to get to where you desire to be, but I genuinely think that Lincoln felt that in order for the American people to have a differing stance, that opinion needed to be based on the Constitution, which is the original source of all of our political power. Our understanding of governance ought to be formed from how we read and interpret the Constitution in a similar way that the Bible guides Christian theology (at least in principle).I believe that if we did this, it would be challenging for our leaders to pass poor legislation and for them to remain in government. But above all, it would be more difficult for them to control our thoughts and feelings about the events happening in our country.

Back to our rock concert, I noticed that several of the songs made allusions to the fact that the United States extends its dominance over the world through its military strength, which culminates in unpleasant consequences. Even though I disagree with Roger Waters' outlook on the United States military, I can't say that I completely disagree with him when it comes to his criticism of how the United States uses and abuses its authority. After the attacks of September 11, it is now more apparent that we did not have the evidence President Bush talked about concerning weapons of mass destruction. This was the primary motivation for invading Iraq once more and attempting to remove Saddam Hussein from power. Looking back on Gulf War II after the attacks of September 11, it is now clear that we did not have this substantiation. However, this is only one aspect of the problem that we brought into Iraq. The country started to break apart when Saddam was driven from power, and in the decades since then, it has grown increasingly influenced by Iran, which is another political foe of the United States.

Because of our actions, there is now a vacuum of authority, and we have been unable to fill it. I will accept that there are times and circumstances in which we should participate in international affairs; nevertheless, there must be a strategy, and there must be a commitment to resolution, for, in the end, we are accountable for the power vacuums that we create. It could be argued that President George W. Bush did not have the authority to attack Iraq a second time under the pretext of those criteria, which we now have strong reasons to believe were erroneous. I would say that the war in Afghanistan was fought for completely different reasons and that the war on terror is necessary, even if it has gone on for twenty years.

After the end of the Vietnam War, when the military draft was abolished, politicians were no longer held to the same degree of political responsibility for the employment of the military or the conflicts in which the United States had been involved. Since the end of the draft, there has been a dramatic rise in the number of incursions that the United States has been a part of all over the world.

These days, presidents commit our country's troops, resources, and billions of dollars overseas whenever they see fit and with little care when November rolls around for an election.

Because of this, I got started writing this. There is a compelling need for change. There have been a lot of talks that the United States may see a second civil war or that western civilization could experience widespread social unrest. I would argue in favor of a different solution, one that may be more difficult to understand but which, in my opinion, results in a better outcome. After all, if we are disgruntled with the carnage that the United States creates in other countries, why would we want to witness the same thing in our own communities? People are not weighing out the consequences of this, or perhaps they did not watch the news over the years, which captured the destruction in Iraq, Afghanistan, former Yugoslavian nations, as well as the nations where we are supporting one side over the other. And in many of these instances mentioned, there are war crimes committed, atrocities that have been ignored or inadequately reported on in a way that keeps us asking questions, but over time we learn nothing. The situation only gets worse the issue in question dissolves from public view.

We cannot allow such reckless behavior to continue. People seem intent on concentrating on the fact that the United States of America has made a lot of blunders these days. We have no option but to face the truth that we have, in the past, engaged in conduct that was not beneficial to us or those around us, whether it was done intentionally or by mistake. But we should also rejoice in the things that we successfully did. There were certain actions that were not the product of wicked intent. When it comes to history, the truth is that both positive and negative events have occurred throughout the course of time. Even decisions that appeared to be reasonable at the time might have unintended consequences farther down the line. The Great Depression was brought on by a number of other factors, but this is only one illustration of what I am trying to explain. After World War One, there was a demand for more grain in Europe, so the United States increased production. As a result, markets eventually adjusted to the increased supply, and prices for grain fell. Many farmers were not making enough money to pay their mortgages, which led to defaults and, among other things, a rush on the banks for their cash. This, in addition to other factors, contributed to the failure of financial institutions and the Great Depression that followed. Although it was not the only factor that led to the Great Depression, this played a significant role in its development. It all started with a need to help individuals who were enduring hardship, but as time went on, there were some unintended outcomes.

The argument is that we should not continue to make the same errors because we have the opportunity to learn from them and change our behavior accordingly. But it's "if" we let ourselves learn from the experience. Therefore, we have the Federal Deposit Insurance Corporation (FDIC), and the government safeguards your bank account for a certain maximum amount.

CHAPTER 05

"By a continuing process of inflation, the government can confiscate, secretly and unobserved, an important part of the wealth of their citizens."

-John Maynard Keynes

I know that I have been straying away from the point I was trying to make. The core argument is that we need change and that change must involve more than just politics. We need a change in our social structure as well. There is no denying that work is a necessity for life, and participation in meaningful occupations is critical to the health and well-being of our society, and participation in meaningful occupations is critical to the health and well-being of our society.

Pay attention to what I have to say before you declare that I have lost my way. We have witnessed, during the course of the 20th century, an increase in the cost of goods, an increase in the compensation of CEOs, an increase in taxes, and an overall increase in the expenses of everything that is necessary for living. The one thing that has not increased, though, is the pay or wages provided to the average worker. No, we have not witnessed this trend in a very, very long time. Even though the affordability of many amenities in life has grown, life still has managed to become increasingly expensive. If you search how much a brand-new automobile cost in the year 1980 and then compare that figure to what it costs now, you will see how much the prices have escalated since then.

To be fair, cars manufactured now offer a lot more conveniences and greater fuel economy than automobiles manufactured 50 years ago did. But let's not forget that the price tag has increased despite the fact that many of those conveniences are now considered common. There are other contributors to the issue, including reckless spending by our political leaders, inflation, and those in positions of power who are aware of how much we depend on cars for transportation and are thus willing to pay a premium for them. In addition, we have witnessed significant increases in the cost of real estate all around the country, particularly during the 1970s. In addition to the myriad of other challenges, this one makes it more difficult for the average American family to make ends meet.

During the times I used to teach young students, I observed that many teenagers devoted a significant amount of time and energy to the requirements of the school as well as the activities that were sponsored by the school. Along with this, families have become increasingly stressed; parents try to keep up with their children to provide opportunities for them and help them in becoming competitive candidates for a good college or university. And here comes another enormity; the stress placed on children to pursue higher education contributes significantly to the growth of student loan debt. The cost of attending higher education institutions continues to rise in tandem with the federal government's efforts to expand the amount of money that college students are eligible to borrow from the government.

When I was a student in the 1980s and 1990s, and when I graduated from college in the middle of the 2000s, the only thing I ever heard was this:

"If you want more opportunities and a better career, go to school for it."

They were undoubtedly correct for a while, but with the financial crisis that occurred in 2007, student loans and college debt, in general, became a matter of widespread attention. When it came to taking on debt to pay for education, people's opinions changed, and today, in the year 2022, we constantly hear about student loan amnesty and how much it is required or how much it is hated depending on who you talk to. If the government cancels the loans, then the cost will be passed on to the individual taxpayers. This would not be fair to those people who have already paid off their education debt or found other ways to avoid it. On the other hand, nobody owned a crystal ball at the time of taking loans. Thus it was impossible to precisely anticipate the results of the economy years in advance.

It seems to me that people are not focusing their attention on the most important aspect of the issue quite enough. People have a valid reason to be worried about the large amounts of tax money that are being spent, but why do we not hold universities and colleges accountable for the outrageous price tag? The majority of these educational institutions are nonprofits, and I believe that they make use of their tax-exempt status in order to preserve their financial resources. When you analyze how expensive universities and colleges are, you will find it hard to believe that such a basic necessity for young people is emptying their pockets to such an extent. We are not even discussing the income that colleges earn from the sale of athletic apparel and the money generated by the schools' sports activities.

It is not a bad thing for them to make money; nevertheless, it is likely that they have gone too far by allowing their cost of attendance to become excessively expensive. There are not too many of my students that are planning to continue their education after high school these days. Since there could be less of a demand in this area, change may occur sooner whether those concerned like it or not.

Efficiency is an additional factor that impacts the lives of the average worker. The average worker has become significantly more productive as a result of the technical advancements that have occurred over the course of the last five decades. However, they are not compensated for any of the increased productivity. Think back to how things were under COVID— we were able to engage in videoconferencing and distant learning, and people were able to work from the comfort of their own homes thanks to the advantages offered by the internet. When you think about it as a teacher, it is hard to believe that there was ever a period when everything had to be recorded on paper, computed by hand, and all of that other amazing things. These days, I conduct most of my work on a computer, and it saves me a significant amount of time. Imagine someone who worked in an office in 1970; although they had access to a phone, they had to rely on the mail to communicate with coworkers and clients. In addition to that, you had to wait for a response. These days, you can have a full discussion using facetime or whatever else is available on your phone anyplace in the world where your phone will operate in real-time. We are capable of accomplishing a great deal more now than people were capable of doing fifty years ago. Despite this, we continue to adhere to a 5-day work week and put in around 40 hours each week.

Does that sound progressive to you? At all? I mean, what's the point of all that advancement if a person still has to work like a robot 9-5 a day?

Our professions have the potential to be quite admirable; I have a great deal of respect for physicians, attorneys, and others whose work requires significant dedication to the time spent in the office and who contribute to the smooth operation of our society. Maybe we have developed an unhealthy obsession with and respect for this. When I worked with some individuals in the past, I realized that they prefer to be at work, not necessarily because they enjoy their work, but rather because their employment serves as an escape from the reality that they have created for themselves outside of work. It's very likely that all of us, at some point in our lives, have shared this sentiment or that at least one of our friends or family members does. When we do this, when we make ourselves endlessly available at work, it seems to me that we are depriving ourselves of opportunities in other areas of our lives. Since there are only 24 hours in a day, you need to plan out how you will spend each of those hours.

Since we are in need of money, there are occasions when we are required to stay late at work willingly and not because our supervisor makes us. It would appear that in our modern culture, an increasing number of us are in need of a second job, longer workdays, or both in order to bring in enough money to cover our expenses. When you choose to do this, you are engaging in a great deal of labor, which brings to mind what we discussed in part on increasing productivity. If the average worker was paid better and had access to better benefits, more people could make a choice to be at home for dinner. This would give them the opportunity to spend some much-needed time with their families or loved ones and help to strengthen their relationships.

I have listened to my pupils about their families, the relationships they have with them, and their life at home. After hearing about their experiences, I believe it might be challenging for them to refrain from passing judgment on their parents based on the choices they made by them. If there is one thing that teachers would agree on, it is our students' lack of respect for authority figures, as well as their inability to concentrate and control their conduct. Unfortunately, these issues have been on the rise in recent years. I believe much of this comes from the experiences kids have at home. There is an overwhelming number of parents who, for various reasons, are unable to be there when their children need them due to their demanding work schedules or other commitments that interfere with their availability. We need to make changes in our society so that parents have the opportunity to spend quality time with their children, not so that they can help their children with their homework, but so they can engage in activities that help them bond as a family and pursue other interests that are important to them.

I acknowledge that I probably come off as extremist, and you may believe that I am opposed to western ideologies or capitalism; however, this is not the case. I think that individuals should not only be capable of making money and becoming successful individually, but they should also be willing to let others succeed. I want to go back to what I was saying before, the efficiency of the average worker, to explain why there is a major problem with the salaries that people are getting. What other options do you have besides passing laws to make this different? When we get our government engaged, we have a tendency to create headaches and spend more money than we need should. Turning to legislation appears to create more difficulties because you get the government involved.

The solution to this predicament is a more difficult one. I am of the belief that we must persuade those working in higher-level business positions to adjust the criteria by which they evaluate a company's level of financial performance. In most cases, there is a pie chart, and if you take away from one slice, such as profits, they will often compensate by reducing expenditures in another area to make up the difference. The existence of financial ambitions or expectations for profits on the part of shareholders and CEOs is a contributory factor to the development of this problem. For them, you are not performing better this year if you are not making more money than you did in the previous year. There are those who will argue that this is what capitalism is. In my view, this is nothing more than an attempt to increase one's wealth through pure greed and nothing else. A capitalist is someone who holds the belief that consumers and sellers should be able to freely engage with and participate in the market; however, being a capitalist does not mean that you continuously make enormous profits.

Many people's concepts of what it means to be a capitalist have, in my opinion, been tainted by the greed that has been prevalent in our country, and as a result, many people now believe that capitalism is more similar to a malignancy. It is time for us to stop praising or rewarding those in positions of authority and motivated by greed. It is a problem that has persisted for a long time. However, the problem is more complex because who am I to tell anyone else that they are being greedy?

In Western Civilization, our ethics and sense of morality have been taught to us by religion, regardless of whether or not we are willing to recognize this fact. We have undervalued religion as our society has gotten more secular, but when it comes to matters of ethics and morals, I would say that they have not been replaced by anything else. This is something I can advocate for. The vast majority of religious philosophies convey the message that greed is immoral, particularly when it comes at the expense of another person. Regardless, our society has evolved to the point where there are many principles of a free market in existence, but there is very little emphasis placed on the cultivation of self-control and the renunciation of greed.

Since it goes against the fundamental tenets of most religious ideologies, it is impossible for me, as a religious person, to ever coerce another person into being religious. People who want it can be inspired, encouraged, and assisted, but using force is not the right way. I believe that in this matter, it is the same; we cannot let the government make this decision for us. Instead, we must work to create a society in which people care about one another. We need to change the way we look at one another as well as the way we define success. That's one way to solve the compensation problem among workers.

I want to make it quite clear that I do not think there is anything particularly wrong with being wealthy. We have witnessed a great number of people in the United States achieve great success and change the course of history. However, there is most likely a great deal more that we are capable of doing in terms of compensating individuals who work for us and how we treat them in general. While some in higher circles and with greater status are rewarded substantially in ways that the majority of us can only dream of, many people in the United States are working long hours today and receiving wages that are not enough to meet the needs of their families. These changes have to originate from the people, not from the interference of the government. When the government gets involved, it almost always results in new legislation, new laws, new taxes, and new authorities, among other things, but nothing that makes it easier for people.

There are so many new rules and regulations issued every year that it gives the impression that those who become wealthy develop a sense of paranoia and strive to prevent others from attaining the same degree of success as they have. Because of this, I have the feeling that our country is no longer a truly capitalist nation. If we want to call ourselves capitalists, we need to eliminate the excessive amounts of government intervention, regulation, and taxes that exist in our system. A significant portion of the population of the world does not have access to the free-market economy in the same way that we have. In addition, I would say that there is a growing consensus that Americans are losing the opportunity to participate and prosper in the economic system that we have here in the United States.

CHAPTER 06

*"We have lots of studies about what's wrong with our education system.
We need to accept responsibility, be bold, find solutions, and move
forward to make education a centerpiece of our economic development."*

— Christine Gregoire

I couldn't agree more with the statement made by Christine
Gregoire here. Throughout this book, the one thing that has
been a constant part of my discussion, regardless of the
problem being discussed, is the information. Education, if
provided properly and through authentic means, is one of the
biggest sources of information.

But what happens if the education system itself is corrupted in
terms of getting individuals overworked? What consequences
does it have on the economy as a whole?

In light of the fact that knowledge serves as the foundation for
all economic systems, there is an essential connection between
the educational system and the economic system and its
growth. It is critical to meaningfully integrate these two
systems in order for management to realize the goal of
improved collaboration between both systems.

Why?

Because despite the need for education for a prospering
economy, we can't neglect the fact that people do need some
time off work and school to have quality time with families.

I want to connect the issue of economics with our struggles
dealing with the pressures that attending school and living a
normal life put on us. Imagine for a moment if individuals were

paid more, had better benefits that assisted them in leading healthier lives, and had access to the proper medical care and prevention. Imagine, on top of this, if individuals had more time to do things with their families, to join college programs that they have always desired to enroll in, to study that foreign language that they have always wanted to learn, or just to relax from their hectic schedules.

It seems too good to be true, doesn't it? To put things into perspective, it's not as if doing so would be an insurmountable task. An opportunity like this is a fundamental human right that belongs to each and every person, and this fact should not come as a surprise to anybody. Everyone should be given the opportunity to make their life better, and having access to educational opportunities is one of the most crucial factors in making that a reality.

Perhaps our next big leap forward in society will happen when we are able to balance out work, family, and free time in our lives. I think that we are asking too much of families these days with more taxes and an increased need for extracurricular activities and sports after school. I completely agree that all of these things are important to assist the child in becoming a competitive applicant for a top institution or college. But I still believe that a healthy balance between school/work and personal life is crucial to building a truly progressive society. Why does everyone have to work extra hours and give up family time in exchange for making more money just so they can live a comfortable life?

"Schools are in many ways perhaps the first step in getting us to understand that institutions control our lives and that we should accept unquestionably that there can be no objection to this."

— Mango Wodzak

Do families still regularly gather around the dinner table? As our society continues to adapt to the conditions and expectations that are now in place, it is possible that, in the not-too-distant future, dinner tables and dining rooms may become smaller. My family life while I was growing up was by no means ideal, but we did sit down to eat together as a family every night until we were all adults and our schedules made it more difficult to do so.

In retrospect, my family began to grow more distant when we no longer had consistent dinner times with everyone present. As a teacher, I am privy to the sentiments of many parents towards their children, and I can say with certainty that they look forward to the month of January and August when the children resume their academic schedules. However, family time needs to be a sacred thing. If blood family is not available, we should make time for those who are considered family. I am of the opinion that a huge proportion of the societal issues that have been plaguing our country could be avoided or, at the very least, alleviated if we placed a greater emphasis on setting aside time each evening for family dinner or some other form of family time when parents and children come together to interact and hopefully enjoy a hearty meal.

But again, this would certainly be challenging for a lot of people. The fact that we are always so busy is currently a major problem for us. We have far too many distractions! We are constantly inundated with new things to watch online, new movies to see in cinemas, new sports events, after-school programs, games, and performances for our children, and many other things. We need to figure out a way to make our evenings more calm and peaceful so that we have time to catch up and get ready for the next day. I also think that this would help us cope with our worry and stress, which for many of us, seems to be never-ending. We have to reclaim some of our time and priorities, spending it with our families and other important people in our lives.

It's quite clear that it won't work like magic. We cannot wave a magic wand and expect everything to fall into place overnight. It will take some time, and it is quite unlikely that many people will accept it. But, if we want to see a change in the world, we need to be willing to make the change ourselves and set the example that we want to see around us. More individuals will be willing to accept the change and make the necessary adjustments if more and more families make the decision to withdraw from the outside world for a while so they can spend time doing what truly matters. We also need to keep in mind that the United States is a nation comprised of many different cultures, each of which most likely has its own conception of what constitutes a family, what constitutes meals, and so on. The very definition of family varies from culture to culture, some will define it as blood exclusively, and others might have a large family with almost no blood relations present. We will most likely see the effects of the changes we make in our houses reflected in the world around us; for this reason, we need to make positive changes in our homes. The goal here is to get everyone talking again, to get their thoughts and feelings out in the open, and not to impose our will on other people.

If we keep doing what we have been doing, there will come a time when we will merely be robots working for survival and deprived of the love of a family. We need an education system that supports the notion of having time for our families. We need an education system that effectively provides us the knowledge and skill to earn better and not just divide our schedule into so many activities that eat up our days. Let's not make education systems a way to control people's lives but rather a way to equip them with enough to strive for a better life.

If we don't change things today, there will come a time that we will be working all day just to make money and still won't have enough to live a comfortable life. It will be prohibitively expensive for the average person to buy a home, receive higher education, and there will be an excessive number of people who will be unable to become entrepreneurs as a result of government regulations. The ultimate result would be an individual person becoming a typical American; impoverished, ignorant, and dependent on the government.

There has to be a way to level the playing field for everyone without resorting to handouts or depleting all of our available financial resources in the process. I wish I had solutions for these kinds of problems, but I think the first thing we need to do is start talking about them, and then we will start moving in the right direction.

CHAPTER 07

I will continue the discussion by addressing the significance of education, but more importantly, the significance of quality education and the components that go into creating it.

To begin, I will throw in a bitter fact; our educational system is a mess. The primary purpose of public schools nowadays is that of a daycare center, with education taking a distant second place. This is a problem and desperately needs to be fixed. In addition to being regarded as pointless, children and their parents frequently regard school as a burdensome but unavoidable obligation that should be endured but should not be taken seriously.

As a teacher, I have observed that wonderful things transpire whenever a child's parents take an interest in the activities that take place at school. During their time in high school, I have seen some truly remarkable kids making tremendous strides in both their personal and academic development. On the other hand, I have also witnessed numerous kids cruise through the system with little to no progress in either area. It is really disheartening to see such a huge number of youngsters reaching adulthood while still being mentally trapped in their teenage years. To begin, parents have a lot on their plates. Most parents are preoccupied with their careers or other obligations, which keeps them from being involved in their children's education and the experiences they have in school.

Another problem that stems from problems at home is that there are many who rely on public schools to teach their kids things like morality, ethics, and behavior to their children. For whatever reason, whether it be that they are a single parent at home, have multiple jobs, or have a troubled relationship with their teenage child in general, they fail to pay attention to the good upbringing of their children. In my opinion, this is a rather precarious situation that most of us find ourselves in right now as a society. We are placing more and more responsibilities on educators while also devaluating public schools in general. Kids need to have that talk with their parents or another trusted adult about what they learn and learn how to assign value to the things they learn so that they may form both their character and their perspective of the world with the guidance of an adult. Kids will go to the internet, popular culture characters, and other children their age to help them put what they learn into perspective if there is no adult there to guide them. When they reach high school, I find a lot of children lacking basic values and beliefs that the majority of adults have today, regardless of whether they are religious or not. We only blame the new generation for being spoilt or disrespectful without looking at the reasons behind their behaviors.

Sadly, public education is at the mercy of politics, and if you have politicians who support education, you have, in most cases, better funding for schools, although you likely have higher property taxes. There has to be a more effective method of funding schools that does not place the burden on property owners. Politicians need to find other ways in which our public schools can be funded, free of political influences in terms of knowledge provided and should demonstrate their support for teaching staff by giving them a greater say in the curricula that are used in their respective societies.

In addition to this, I believe that there is one major component that would benefit practically every single teacher out there, and that is for parents to become involved in the activities that their children are participating in while they are attending school. Not only for behavioral reasons, which are incredibly useful, but also talk to your children about what they are learning in school and why they are learning it. This will help them make better choices in their everyday lives. Even if you don't think a certain topic is all that important to you, the information that you are taught in school is there for a reason. If you teach your children how to organize the information that they take in, it will, at the very least, enable them to participate and work efficiently in the way that they should.

Keep in mind that one of the primary goals of our country's public education system is to assist in molding our children and teenagers in such a way that they are prepared to participate in our Republic as upstanding citizens or something along those lines. But we have to change this. We have to make our children autonomous, so they can make a decision based on their values and morals and not on what they are fed. We need to start somewhere, and at this point, even a slight improvement will make a difference, and it will likely influence others. It will take some time, and perhaps only a certain proportion of our population will make the commitment to participate, but we need to start somewhere.

In my opinion, positive, high-quality change in society takes time, and you can't anticipate rapid change to take place without expecting opposition and unfavorable responses from people. Something negative happens when we push people to change in the way we want. To avoid this, you need to inspire others to make the change you desire because you can't make them do it against their will. If you want it to be genuine and long-lasting, you have to show its positive impact through your actions.

My thoughts turn to the pandemic and how frequently we were provided with new regulations that, in many instances, were not even followed by the leadership of our institutions. How can we expect everyone else in society to make the change if we are not willing to make the change ourselves?

Keep in mind that it is important for us to show concern for the rights of the individual. But at the same time, we must refrain from reacting emotionally to the challenges we are currently confronted with. Even if we could all agree that our society has problems that need to be corrected, we might not all agree on the best way to address those problems. When we are impatient and decide that we need significant change right away, we infringe on the rights of other people and create negative pressure on people, leading some of them to choose to act out rather than try to see that point of view. If anything, I hope this work will spark discussion and get people talking about how we can make things better.

"I cannot help fearing that men may reach a point where they look at every new theory as a danger, every innovation as a toilsome trouble, every social advance as a first step toward revolution and that they may absolutely refuse to move at all."

— Alexis de Tocqueville

Let's not become the ones making societal progress a far-fetched and impossible dream. Become an example of inspiration and even if people fear your notions, step forward and prove them wrong because this change is not just about us but the generations to come.

CHAPTER 08 | CONCLUSION

As a backdrop, I have focused on the most significant problems facing our society, as well as how those problems have impeded our advancement as a country. We are aware of the things that require change, but the ultimate question remains unanswered; HOW?

How do we put an end to all of these problems? I really wish I knew the answers. The capacity to recognize that there is an issue is one that I've developed from consistently looking at things from a different angle and changing my viewpoint. However, as far as creating a workable solution goes, I can say that any of us have succeeded in finding one. And that's the tougher step.

We need to change just the same! It will not be an easy task, and it is inevitable that we will continue to argue with one another as we try to figure out where to begin and what to do along the way. This will make the process more difficult. Nevertheless, I believe that if we put in the effort, we are capable of accomplishing something truly remarkable.

This ties into what I was saying before about preventing a second civil war or some other sort of civil unrest from breaking out in the country. I am of the opinion that a renaissance is what we are actually hoping for. We need an American Renaissance, in which we return to the original philosophies that inspired the institution of our country and government, possibly readjusting some of the concepts to our modern times rather than resorting to violence. The idea of resorting to violence reminds me more of the expression "throwing the baby out with the bath water," an idiomatic term referring to a preventable error in which something useful or of value is destroyed in the process of trying to get rid of something undesired.

Although there are flaws with our government and our legal system has significant challenges, we still have a lot in place that are operating well.

Despite all the odds, I firmly believe that our Constitution should be preserved. In order for it to work, we need to play our part; we need to take ownership of it and actually live by it. Instead of relying on other people to interpret it for us, I believe that we take it upon ourselves to study and understand it. Only then will we be equipped enough to make wise and informed decisions.

This might seem like a huge task to many, but to understand the Constitution, you do not need to be a genius. However, you do need to have some form of formal education, to understand the language of the laws. But even before that, you have the will. You need constantly remind yourself why you are putting so much effort into understanding it. Remind yourself that if we want to be able to effectively hold our political leaders responsible for their actions, we, the people, need to make this a top priority. At the very least, it is a starting point.

Although it is not within our power to cure everything, we have the ability to ignite the spark, and the generations who come after us will play their part in fanning the flames into a raging firestorm that will consume all of the failings of society in its wake. We can begin by getting our thoughts in the right place. When we have a better understanding of how our government is supposed to function, we will be in a better position to choose the people who will run it. We will have the ability to determine whether candidates for public office are qualified for the positions for which they are competing. When it comes to other concerns, such as term limits, the formation of legislation, and the money from lobbyists, there is little doubt that these are matters that need to be addressed. These concerns, in particular, have been a source of contention. However, a society that has successfully developed a foundation on how our government is supposed to work will be in a better position to address these problems when they arise. Once there, we can start working on the changes required from the vantage point of having more information at our disposal.

The Constitution has much to offer, and there are many philosophical concepts from 1787 that people will focus on that I am not suggesting we should. For instance, during the time when the Constitution was being established, women did not have the right to vote, and going back to that mindset is not something that I am advocating for. The principle of egalitarianism is the one that I care most about seeing revived in the United States of America. However, this concept was only applied at certain levels, and it was definitely not applied to Native Americans or African Americans. This concept was a part of the heritage, and it was a part of America very early on in its history. What if, though, we gave it another shot? What would happen if we tried to live by the principle that everyone is equal, despite differences in sexual orientation, religious beliefs, racial background, and political ideologies? What if some of the rules that are currently in place were relaxed, and we enabled more individuals to engage in our economic system to the fullest extent possible?

While thinking about the Constitution, I am drawn to the Preamble:

We, the people of the United States, in Order to form a more perfect Union, establish Justice, insure domestic Tranquility, provide for the common defense, promote the general welfare, and secure the Blessings of Liberty to ourselves and our Posterity, do ordain and establish this Constitution for the United States.

There are many criticisms about the founding fathers today, but I've always found it intriguing that the Preamble started off with the three words "we the people." This has a profound impact on me since it speaks of all of us together as one. It does not express anything about classes, religious groups, or other distinct groups of people in this passage; rather, it simply refers to the people who live in the United States of America in its entirety. Perhaps we need to start thinking this way again. It is important that we regard one another as fellow citizens of the Republic. After all, we are all a part of this together, and it is only when we cooperate with one another that we are able to make things operate the way they are intended to. You may argue that people did not think this way in the past due to racism or prejudice. But now, there is nothing keeping us from changing the way we think and aligning it with the core of our Constitution; we are all one people. We have to stop regarding ourselves as separate entities and come to terms with the fact that the qualities that bind us together are unique and more powerful than the ones that set us apart from one another.

It may sound like a fairytale, but for many people who came to this country, America WAS a fairytale. For many of us, living here was like a dream come true. You do not have to embrace someone's choices and lifestyle, but you are liberated to allow them to follow their dreams and ambitions in life. You are able to let them seek the life, liberty, and happiness of their choosing. I am aware that this notion gets tossed around a lot in our society, and as we have seen, it has also become tougher for our nation to figure out who has equal access to the law.

The solution, although it may be difficult for some people to embrace, is for each of us to have equal access to the protection that our laws provide. Egalitarianism could terrify some individuals. After all, in 1789, there was not nearly as much diversity in the lifestyles that are present now. People might be concerned, for instance, that offering equality to everyone, regardless of the lifestyle choices they choose, could lead to the legalization of everything and everything. This would not be the case since it is illegal to violate the rights of other people. As a result, any organizations that aim to take anything away from other people would not be tolerated. It is not lawful to violate the rights or privileges of anybody who is guaranteed those rights or privileges by the Constitution of the United States. My impression is that many are reluctant to accept others for who they truly are because they believe that doing so would constitute the implicit approval of such individuals. It is important to keep in mind that the United States of America is a blending pot nation comprised of people from a diverse array of ethnicities and cultural traditions who frequently find themselves working alongside one another. And in some instances, living together. Although it may take some time to sort out, I do believe we can do it.

If we are serious about making changes to the United States of America, then I believe what we need is a renaissance and not just a fresh start for the entire country. I believe that we need to begin with ourselves; as people, we need to change. We need to make it a priority to learn as much as we can about the documents that govern our community and have more meaningful conversations with our neighbors. We must not only listen to our friends and family but also to our communities. We must do everything we can to make them feel as though they are also a part of the American Dream. We have been given so much; it would be a shame to let it fall apart.

We as a people need to return back to our roots. Despite the fact that we are such a diverse community, there are some things that all of us can agree on, such as the right to be happy, liberty, and freedom. It is inevitable that there will be points of contention, particularly in regard to the resolution of issues. However, if we can keep in mind that we are all equally important components of this Republic and respect each other along with our unique characteristics, I believe that we will be able to find a solution to the problem. If we keep in mind that each of us deserves equal protection under the law, that we are all entitled to the protection of the Constitution, that it does not apply to one group more than another, and that we are all equal partakers in it, then we will truly have a Republic we can be proud of.

Most importantly, we will be able to provide a future for our children. You know what to do about it. You know how to make it a reality. You and each one of us have to embrace what was bound to keep us together as a nation; Our Constitution. And we can only ensure its implication through pure determination to defend it.

"The strength of the Constitution lies entirely in the determination of each citizen to defend it. Only if every single citizen feels duty bound to do his share in this defense are the constitutional rights secure."

– Albert Einstein

Made in the USA
Las Vegas, NV
31 January 2023

66571666R00033